In Control:

Learning to Say No to Sexual Pressure

Sexual pressure can be confusing and scary.

The Teen Pregnancy Prevention Library

In Control:
Learning to Say No to Sexual Pressure

by Anna Kreiner

THE ROSEN PUBLISHING GROUP, INC.
NEW YORK

Published in 1997 by The Rosen Publishing Group, Inc.
29 East 21st Street, New York, NY 10010

First Edition

Library of Congress Cataloging-in-Publication Data

Kreiner, Anna.
    In control : learning to say no to sexual pressure / Anna Kreiner.
      p. cm. — (The teen pregnancy prevention library)
    Includes bibliographical references and index.
    Summary: Discusses different kinds of sexual pressure and considers ways young people can negotiate with their partners and determine their own values and ethics regarding sex.
    ISBN 0-8239-2248-0
    1. Sexual ethics for teenagers—Juvenile literature.
2. Teenagers—Sexual behavior—Juvenile literature. 3. Peer pressure in adolescence—Juvenile literature. [1. Sexual ethics.
2. Youth—Sexual behavior. 3. Peer pressure.] I. Title.
II. Series.
HQ35.K68 1996
306.7'0835—dc20   95-40057
                                                CIP
                                                  AC

Manufactured in the United States of America

Contents

Introduction

KEVIN AND NINA HAD BEEN DATING FOR SIX MONTHS. *They had fooled around a little bit but never gone all the way. Nina was getting nervous. Yesterday Kevin told her that if she really loved him, she would sleep with him. Nina didn't think she was ready to have sex yet, but she didn't want to lose Kevin either. What should she do?*

Steven and Luis sat in the locker room getting ready for the big game. Steven told Luis about his new girl-friend. "Rosann is the coolest girl in the world. I really love her."

"Have you two done it yet?" asked Luis.

"No," Steven said. "I don't want to ask her to do that yet."

"Give me a break!" said Luis. "What kind of a guy are you? Everyone knows you're not really a man until you've had sex. Besides, I've heard Rosann is pretty easy, if you know what I mean."

Steven knew he didn't want to have sex before he

got married. But what would his friends think if they knew that? And he felt really sick at his friend's suggestion that his girlfriend was a pushover.

Having a boyfriend or girlfriend can be an exciting experience. The two of you really like each other. You may go to the movies or sports events or just hang out together. Some people also enjoy hugging or kissing their partners. You may become curious about getting more involved sexually.

You may love your boyfriend or girlfriend. But he or she may pressure you to go further sexually than you want to go. This is sexual pressure. You may be asked to do things that make you uncomfortable, such as kissing, touching, or sexual intercourse.

Engaging in sexual activity can have serious, long-term consequences, so you should consider carefully what you are doing. You need to make important decisions about your sexual actions and think about their consequences.

You may already be in a relationship and have begun to make choices. But even if you don't have a boyfriend or girlfriend yet, it is a good idea to prepare yourself.

In fact, it may be very useful to think about these issues now, before you start feeling sexual pressure. Use this opportunity to think about how you really feel. Anyone who chooses to become

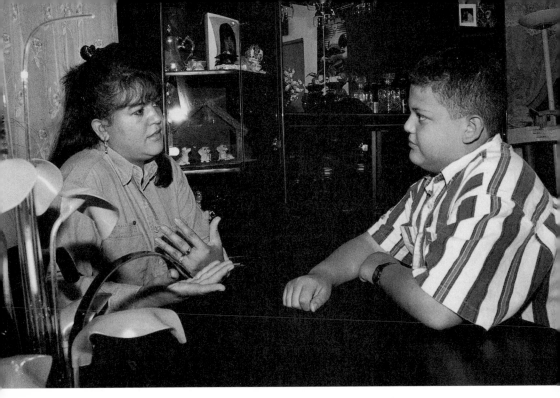

Talk with a parent or older friend about your feelings if you are confused about sexual pressure.

involved in a relationship should consider these
important questions:

- How far are you willing to go sexually?
- What makes you feel uncomfortable?
- How would your parents feel if they found out
  you were sexually involved with someone?
- Will you lose your partner if you say no?
- What happens if you say yes to sex?
- Are you ready to become a parent?
- What about the risk of sexually transmitted dis-
  eases such as AIDS (for which there is no cure)?

You should have a clear idea of your sexual
values and your limits—and how you plan to stay
true to them if you enter into a relationship. If you

know your limits beforehand, it will be easier to say no to sexual activity that makes you feel uncomfortable.

Sexual pressure comes in many forms. This book will help you to recognize sexual pressure and learn how to say no to it. You can still enjoy dating without having to do anything that doesn't feel right.

Dealing with sexual pressure is a challenge. You may feel like others will look down on you for saying no, or think that your partner will reject you. But there are many ways to say no and maintain both your relationship and your self-respect. If you know how to stay in control, you will feel better about yourself in the long run. Remember, it's *you* who are involved in the relationship—not just your body.

This book gives you the opportunity to look at your own values and decide how far you are willing to go. You'll learn about the different kinds of sexual pressure and how you can negotiate with your partner.

Sometimes saying no may seem difficult or scary, but it will help you in the long run. You'll have higher self-esteem and more confidence. You won't suffer the negative consequences of sexual behavior, such as pregnancy and disease. And you will be the one who remains in control of your own life.

Teens may be more likely to put sexual pressure on their partners if their friends make fun of them for not having sex.

1 Establishing Your Values and Setting Limits

*"**My boyfriend told me that I would have sex** with him if I loved him. I do love him, but I also know that I don't want to have sex before I get married,"* said Susan. *"I decided that if he really loved me, he would respect my choices. I don't want to be in a relationship with someone who won't honor my decisions."*

"I'm not ready to have sex yet. My religion taught me that you should wait until you get married," said Richard. "So I'm not going to stay with anyone who pressures me to get involved sexually."

"Having sex with someone is a big commitment. And I don't want to do it with just anyone," said Rosa. "I'm going to wait until I'm married or in a long-term relationship.

"I'm not ready for sex yet. I don't want to get pregnant or get AIDS. I'm way too young to be a mother, and I'm scared of sexually transmitted disease. So I'm going to wait."

How do you feel about your own sexual behavior? What is important to you? What do you think is appropriate in a relationship?

Think about your values—your beliefs about what is right and wrong—before you get involved. Then you can make decisions that will feel right to you.

Many people believe that sex outside of marriage is wrong. You may have grown up in a family with strong religious beliefs. Many of these families think teens should wait until they are married before they have sex.

But many teens from nonreligious families also think that having sex now is not right for them. They have chosen sexual abstinence. People who are abstinent do not engage in sexual intercourse.

When you are a teenager, you go through many physical and emotional changes. You are still learning about your body and your relationships with other people. For many teens this is a time of exploration, and they are not yet ready to have sex.

Is It Worth It?
Sexual intercourse can be a healthy part of a committed relationship between mature, responsible people. Many people choose to put off having that special experience until they are sure they have found the right person. They decide to wait until

Risky sexual activity can lead to pregnancy and sexually transmitted diseases.

Some teens meet in discussion groups to encourage each other to remain abstinent.

they are in a long-term relationship or are married before they engage in sexual activity.

You may think that your current boyfriend or girlfriend is the person you will be with forever, but feelings can change. The person you are dating now may not be the person you marry or decide to stay with for the rest of your life. So now may not be a good time for you to get involved in serious sexual activity, especially considering the possible consequences of unsafe sexual practices: sexually transmitted diseases (STDS), including AIDS, and unwanted pregnancy.

"My cousin got pregnant during her senior year of high school. She was going to go to college, but now she

has to stay home with the baby. She doesn't know if she'll ever be able to go back to school. I don't want that to happen to me, so I'm definitely saying no to sex now," said Kendra.

"I can't believe my girlfriend got pregnant. I thought having sex would prove I was a real man," said Roberto. "The only thing I know now is that real men have to support their kids. And I sure wasn't ready to be a father yet."

"I had sex with a boy I didn't know very well. We were at a big party, and both of us had had too much to drink. I never saw him again. But I'll never forget him. Thanks to our night together, I got herpes," said Marla. "I'll have to live with that reminder for the rest of my life."

The idea of having sex may be exciting, but you should remember that sex can complicate a relationship. You are taking on a new responsibility. It is important to think about the effects of your actions before you make any decisions about sex.

Sexual activity can have physical consequences. You run the risk of contracting many serious sexually transmitted diseases—such as chlamydia, gonorrhea, herpes, syphilis, or AIDS—by having unprotected sex. AIDS is a fatal disease for which

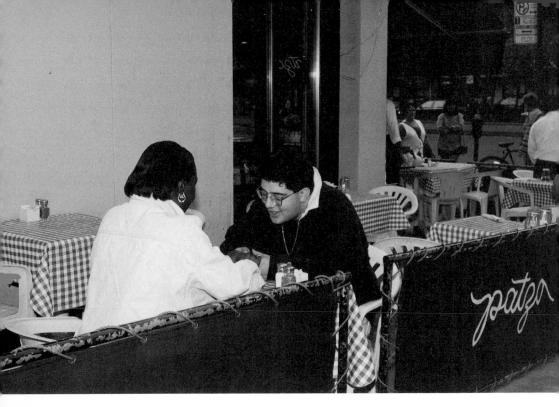

Staying within your boundaries might mean meeting your dates at public places.

there is no cure. It is passed from an infected person to someone else by the exchange of bodily fluids such as semen, blood, and vaginal secretions.

Even if you have sex only once or only during certain times of the month, you or your partner could get pregnant. You can get pregnant the first time you have sex.

You may not know your partner's sexual history. If you become sexually involved with this person, you are taking a major risk. Are you willing to take that risk? The only way you can be sure of avoiding the consequences of sexual activity is by being abstinent.

We have mentioned only a few reasons why

some people choose not to have sex. Do you have other reasons for not engaging in sex?

Once you know what is important to you, you will be able to make wise decisions about your sexual behavior. The first step is to determine clearly in your mind what you think is appropriate behavior for you.

Setting Boundaries

Once you have established your values, you should set your boundaries.

How far are you willing to go sexually? Some teens are comfortable with holding hands. Eventually you may want to hug and kiss. It's normal to have feelings of affection for your boyfriend or girlfriend and to want to express them. But there are ways to do this without "going all the way."

It is a wise idea to talk with your partner about your boundaries. If each of you has a clear understanding of how far you are willing to go, you will be less likely to encounter sexual problems later.

Luisa and Cal had been friends since elementary school. In high school Cal asked Luisa to go with him to the junior prom.

Then they decided that they wanted to go steady.

"We talked early on about how far each of us was willing to go," says Luisa.

"I knew that there was no way I was going to get involved sexually. I was very clear in my own mind that I was going to limit my sexual activity.

"I told Cal that if he tried to push me beyond my limits, I would end the relationship. I really like him, but I need someone who is willing to respect my choices.

"He listened to what I said and agreed to respect my decisions.

"We've been dating for six months, and Cal has never asked me to do anything that didn't feel right.

"The key was laying out the boundaries early. That way I knew we'd be less likely to run into trouble later."

"Patti kept asking me to have sex," said Bill. "I told her I wasn't ready to sleep with her. I don't want to become a father, and I really believe in waiting until I get married.

"I thought we could keep going out even though we disagreed. But when she told me she wouldn't see me anymore if I didn't sleep with her, I decided to end the relationship.

"I'll miss her, because I like her as a person. But I don't want a girlfriend who won't respect my choices. If she keeps trying to put sexual pressure on me, I know she doesn't really care about my feelings."

Set your limits before you get involved in a relationship. Sometimes, in the heat of the moment, it is hard to think clearly. You may love being with your partner. But remember that your actions will have consequences. Think carefully before you engage in sexual activity.

If you set your limits early in the relationship, you won't have to worry about mixed signals later. And you can be sure of maintaining your values even when you are faced with sexual pressure. Learning to say no will help you stay in control.

2 Kinds of Sexual Pressure

SONDRA AND DAN HAD A GREAT TIME AT THE
movies. Now they were walking in the park at night.
Sondra really liked holding hands with Dan and was
pretty excited when he started to kiss her. But when he
put his hand inside her blouse, she pushed his hand
away. "Come on," said Dan. "I won't hurt you."

"No, Dan," Sondra said firmly. "You're going too
far."

At first Dan was surprised. He thought all girls
wanted to have sex. But when he heard Sondra, he
knew she had clear limits. And he was willing to re-
spect her boundaries.

"Every time I went over to Barbara's house she would
turn down the lights and put sexy music on the stereo.
She told me it would help me 'get in the mood,'" said
Frank. "She kept trying to get me to go to bed with
her. She made me really stress out. I don't want to
have sex with anyone now; I'm too young. I finally
had to stop seeing her. I couldn't take it anymore."

Some teenagers confuse sex with love, and get hurt when the relationship ends.

"The guys on the team kept pushing me to have sex with my girlfriend," said Pat. "So I kept asking her to go further. Neither of us really wanted to sleep together, but I wanted my friends to know I wasn't a wimp. Unfortunately, she got pregnant because we didn't use birth control. I wish I had thought about what I was doing before I started to put pressure on her."

Sexual pressure can take many forms. Anytime someone tries to get you to do something sexually that you don't want to do, he or she is exerting sexual pressure. All sexual pressure is inappropriate. If it makes you uncomfortable, it is wrong. Both boys and girls can exert sexual pressure. Some boys feel that they have to have sex "to be a

Giving in to a partner's pressure not to use birth control can put you at risk for pregnancy.

man." Some girls think having sex will prove their partner really loves them. Sex doesn't equal love. You can still be with and love your partner without doing anything that makes you uncomfortable.

Verbal Sexual Pressure

Some sexual pressure is verbal. Your partner may try to talk you into having sex. But don't let words like "please" make you think that you are being unfair for saying no. If you find yourself arguing with your partner about sexual involvement, it's not a good sign. The decision to have sex is a decision between two people. It is not healthy if you feel you have "given in" to your boyfriend's or girlfriend's desire to have sex.

Your friends may tell you that you should go to bed with your partner. But you're the one who will live with your choice and deal with the consequences—not them.

Pressure Not to Use Birth Control

"Come on, baby," Marco told Lucia. "You said you wanted to have sex. We don't need birth control. Condoms are a drag. I'll make sure you don't get pregnant."

Your partner may try to persuade you not to use birth control, saying that sex is better without it.

You may hear excuses like "It's no fun for me with a condom." Your partner may even try to make *you* feel bad by saying something like, "Don't you think I'm clean? I don't have any diseases!" or "Don't you trust me?"

But unprotected sex can be very dangerous. You may get a sexually transmitted disease, such as AIDS. And there is always the risk of pregnancy, even the first time a couple has sex.

No matter what your partner says, if you do decide to be sexually active, it is vital to protect yourself. Don't let your partner pressure you into having unsafe sex. If someone doesn't care enough about you to protect you from pregnancy and disease, do you really want to become sexually involved with him or her?

Women and men should consult a doctor or counselor to learn about birth control options. The condom is the only form of birth control that prevents against the transmission of sexually transmitted diseases such as AIDS. It protects against the transmission of HIV, which causes AIDS. But if you are sexually active, it is also important to take other precautions to prevent pregnancy. Women may choose to use the birth control pill, the diaphragm, the female condom, Norplant, Depo-Provera, the cervical cap, or spermicidal jellies and foams to provide additional protection. The most effective

Don't let your boyfriend or girlfriend use mind games to change your decision about sex.

protection against pregnancy—besides sexual abstinence—is provided when the condom is used with another method of birth control.

Mind Games

Stephanie and Carlos were in Carlos's living room watching a movie. Carlos moved closer to Stephanie on the sofa and put his arm around her shoulders. "Come on," he said. "We've been dating for six months now. You're just playing games with me, stringing me along. It's time for us to go to bed. How much longer do you think I'm going to put up with this?"

Stephanie began to feel anxious. She loved Carlos, but she wasn't ready for sex. She thought about her friend who had gotten pregnant.

But Stephanie was also afraid Carlos would leave her. Maybe he was right; six months was a long time. Was she being unfair to him?

That night Stephanie told her older sister what had happened.

"Stephanie, it doesn't matter how long you've been dating," said Maria. "You never have to do anything that makes you feel uncomfortable sexually. You're not 'stringing him along.' The two of you can enjoy each other's company without getting involved in sex.

"I think you should talk to Carlos. He's putting sexual pressure on you that you don't need. Don't let him start playing mind games with you. You have to do what you think is right."

Stephanie thought about what Maria had said. She decided her sister was right.

The next day Stephanie told Carlos that she knew her sexual limits—and she wasn't prepared to break them.

At first Carlos was angry. But he thought about what Stephanie had said, and soon he agreed to stop pressuring her. He saw that she wasn't teasing him or doing anything wrong.

In fact, the more he thought about what she said, the more respect he had for her. She knew her own mind, and she wouldn't betray herself just because of his pressure.

"I almost gave in to sexual pressure," said Stephanie. "But I'm glad I said no. I know I did what was right. I stuck to my own boundaries."

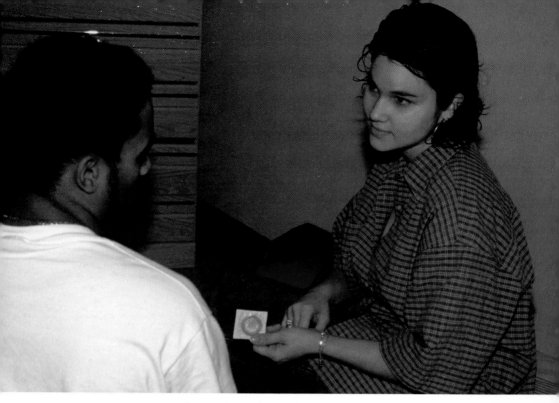

Girls can also put pressure on boys to have sex.

Sometimes people play "mind games" to get you to do what they want. For example, your boyfriend may say that if you love him you will have sex. But that isn't true. You can still love someone and not want to have sex. Sometimes the test of true love is being able to say no. And you will know that he loves you too if he is able to respect the boundaries you have established for yourself.

You always have the right to say no. If any sexual activity feels wrong, you can stop.

Your girlfriend may threaten to leave you if you don't have sex with her. That's another mind game. You don't have to do anything sexually that doesn't feel right. It is up to you to decide whether or not to continue the relationship. Do you want to stay with someone who makes you feel uncomfortable?

"Sally and I liked to walk on the beach at sunset. Usually we held hands. Sometimes we'd kiss good night," said Barry.

"But yesterday she started trying to unzip my pants. I'm not ready to get that close yet."

Physical Pressure

Sometimes sexual pressure becomes physical. Your boyfriend or girlfriend may start exploring your body. Your partner may try to take your clothes off or initiate more physical activity than you want.

You are the one who controls your body. If someone does something to you that you don't like, you have the right to say no.

You also have the right to change your mind. Just because you have sex once doesn't mean you have to have it again. You may decide you want to wait until you're older. And those feelings are perfectly legitimate. You're allowed to change your mind.

Unfortunately, sometimes sexual pressure can become violent.

Rape

Wendy was in tears. "I told him no a thousand times.

If you have been raped, it is very important to report the crime to the police and seek medical help right away.

One time, I said that I had changed my mind. As soon as we started to have sex, I knew it was wrong, and I told him so. But he wouldn't let me stop. He just kept going. He said, 'You just said yes. Now you're saying no. Don't you know what you want?'"

No matter what—no always means no. No one has the right to force you to have sex. Even if you agreed at first, you have the right to change your mind. If your partner forces you even after you have said no—that's rape. Anytime you are forced to have sex against your will, you are a victim of rape. Rape is more than sexual pressure. It is a crime. You have the right to report the person who raped you to the police.

Rape is never your fault, no matter what you were wearing or what you said or what you did. Letting someone hold your hand or kiss you—even going further—does not give him or her the right to have sex with you.

It's important for you to get help if you have been raped. You must report the incident to the police. Talk to a counselor or find a support group. No one deserves to be raped. If you are a victim of rape, you may be frightened and angry. Other people can help you to regain your self-esteem and feel in control of yourself again.

"I let Mark come into my room so we could watch a movie," said Mira, a high school junior. "My parents were out for the night. I didn't think anything would happen because we've done this so many times before. But I was wrong. As soon as the movie started, Mark turned out the lights. Then he forced me to have sex. I begged him like crazy to stop, but he wouldn't."

Unfortunately, date rape is a common problem. Every year thousands of women are raped by men they know. Some men are also the victims of date rape. But many people are afraid to talk about it because they are embarrassed, or they think they deserved what happened to them. Rape is never your fault! Just because you know a person doesn't give him or her the right to have sex with you when you say no.

Even if you've had sex with your boyfriend or girlfriend before, it doesn't give him or her the right to expect sex from you. No matter what, the decision is always yours.

Kissing or fooling around doesn't automatically mean the next stage is sex. Don't let your partner pressure you into having sex "because we've gone this far." You always have the right to say no at any point.

If your partner tries to force you to have sex, you have the right to protect yourself. First try

Don't ruin a happy relationship just because your friends are telling you to have sex.

talking to him or her. If that doesn't work, you may need to be more assertive. Yell for help and try to run away. If you decide to fight, fight with all of your strength; getting away from the person, though, is still your best self-defense.

If you have been raped or had other force used on you, leave the location as soon as possible and get help by calling 911.

Many schools, community centers, and women's groups offer self-defense classes. You might consider enrolling in one of these programs so that you can better protect yourself if sexual pressure becomes physical or violent. *The Get Prepared Library of Violence Prevention for Young Women,* listed at the back of this book, shows you specific techniques for staying safe.

Peer Pressure

"All the girls I know said they couldn't wait to have sex with their boyfriends," said a high school junior.

"I don't want to have sex now. Holding hands and kissing are enough for me. But my friends will think I'm a baby if I don't go all the way. Maybe I should say yes to sex with my boyfriend."

Being a teenager can be a hard time socially. You want to have friends and fit in with the crowd. But having sex when you don't want it will probably make you feel bad about yourself and angry at the people who pressured you.

Dealing with peer pressure is a challenge. You may be afraid that no one will accept you if you don't have sex. But it's important for you to do what you think is right, no matter what.

Sometimes the peer pressure you feel may not even be based in reality. Listen to Ramon's story.

"All of the guys in the locker room used to brag about how they 'scored' with the girls on Saturday night," said Ramon. "But I kept my mouth shut. I thought I was the only one who had never slept with a girl.

"One night my friend Paul and I were talking about

girls. I trust him, so I asked him if I really was the only one who was still a virgin.

"Paul started to laugh. I was afraid he was laughing at me. But do you know what he told me?

"He said that most of the guys on the team hadn't ever slept with a girl. They were just bragging because they wanted to be macho."

You may think that everyone around you is having sex. But that's not true. Many other people your age have decided to say no to sexual intercourse. In a recent survey, 76 percent of the male teens said they thought it was okay to say no to sexual pressure.

Often teens who have had sex wish they had waited. Another survey found that 80 percent of sexually active teen males who were asked the ideal age to start having sex indicated an age older than they were when they first had sex.

The most important part of making sexual choices is to do what seems right for you. It doesn't matter whether or not any or all of your friends are getting involved sexually. The bottom line is that it's your body. Your friends have their own bodies—they shouldn't be telling you what to do with yours.

3 Why Do People Use Sexual Pressure?

SEXUAL PRESSURE IS NEVER RIGHT, NO MATTER what the reason for it. Knowing *why* people exert sexual pressure doesn't make it right, but it may help you figure out effective ways to say no.

Some people think that engaging in sexual activity will improve their relationship. But sexual pressure damages feelings of trust and respect. If you pressure your partner, you show that you don't really care about him or her. If you are not willing to respect your partner's boundaries, you are likely to upset him or her. Your partner may decide to leave the relationship. And even if your partner stays with you, he or she is not likely to feel very comfortable. In the long run, then, sexual pressure won't help you, your partner, or your relationship.

Some teenagers honestly feel that they are ready to have sex. They try to persuade their partners to go along with them—even if their partners don't want sex yet.

But some teens who exert sexual pressure don't

It may seem like everyone is having sex, but this is often not the case.

really want to have sex. They are responding to what they believe society expects of them. They think they have to act in a certain way sexually in order to fit in properly.

Often there are different expectations for males and females in our society. But many of these expectations are based on misinformation.

You should be able to distinguish the facts from the fiction. Then you can stay in control and say no to sexual pressure.

Gender Expectations

Both boys and girls may exert sexual pressure on their partners. But in a good relationship, each partner respects the other's boundaries. It is wrong for a boy to try to force his girlfriend to have sex. And it is just as wrong for a girl to try to persuade her partner to sleep with her if he doesn't want to.

Both boys and girls who believe the myth that "real men have sex" may use sexual pressure on their partners. How can you say no?

If you are a male, remember that being a "real man" doesn't mean you have to be sexually active. You don't need to do anything that makes you uncomfortable just to show you are a man.

You should never try to pressure your partner to have sex. She will not think you are macho if you make her uncomfortable; she is more likely to want to get out of the relationship.

Some girls also think that "real men have sex," and they may try to pressure their partners into having sexual intercourse. If you are a girl, remember that your boyfriend may not want to have sex. You have no right to try to make him act against his beliefs.

If he doesn't want to become close sexually, don't try to force him. You will not be doing anyone any good, and you are likely to put your relationship at risk if you keep pressuring him.

Are your friends bugging you about having sex? Are you afraid they will think less of you if they know you are abstinent? First of all, remember that many of them probably have not had sexual intercourse. And even if they have, you don't have to copy them.

You come first when you make decisions about your sexual behavior. It doesn't matter what anyone else thinks. You must live with yourself and the consequences of your actions.

Also remember that you don't have to discuss your sexual choices with your friends. Your decisions are your own business.

But if you do decide to talk with your friends, you can tell them that you are doing what feels right for you. True friends will respect you for making up your own mind and staying in control of your life. If your peers tease you or make jokes about your choices, they are not real friends. You can find other people who will respect your decisions.

Some men and women think that men and boys should be in control of a relationship. They believe that the male should determine how far both partners go. If you are a woman and you believe this, it may be hard for you to say no to sexual pressure. You may think you have to do what your partner says even if it makes you uncomfortable. And boys who think that men have more power may be more likely to put sexual pressure on their partners.

But this belief is false. Both partners in a relationship are equal. Both of you have a right to stay

It is important to realize that television and movies show sex between young people because "sex sells," not because it is what normal teenagers should do.

in control of your bodies. No man should force a woman to do anything that makes her feel uncomfortable sexually. And a woman always has the right to say no to any form of sexual pressure.

Sexual Pressure in the Media

The movies and television often show couples engaging in sex. This might lead you to think that "everyone is doing it." Prime-time television contains about three sexual acts every hour, usually between unmarried couples.

Television and movie producers include sex scenes because "sex sells." But what you see in the media often isn't realistic.

The characters frequently engage in unsafe sex. One study of daytime television found that fifty hours of programming included 156 sex acts—but mentioned safe sex or birth control only five times.

It is important to remember that television and movies make sex seem exciting, but they often leave out the consequences. In real life, sex isn't always glamorous. You may encounter other messages in the media, in your school, or at home. Before you accept and believe those messages, think about whether they are true. What are they saying about boys and girls and sexual pressure?

4 How to Say No and Stay in Control

"MARTA KEPT TRYING TO PUSH ME INTO HAVING SEX. I wanted to be with her, but I couldn't handle the constant pressure. I got tired of her trying to push me beyond where I felt comfortable," said Sam. "So I finally decided to get out of the relationship. I'm much happier now. Someday I'd like to have another girlfriend, but for now I'd rather be alone than be with someone who makes me uncomfortable."

"I really love Michael, but one thing about him drove me crazy," said a high school student. "We went to the movies together every Saturday. And every time we left he would try to get me to go home and go to bed with him.

"I thought a long time about my feelings and whether or not I wanted to stay with him. I talked to my mom and my sister. Finally I decided that I wanted to be with him, but only if he would respect my boundaries.

"We had a long talk, and he agreed to stop the pressure. I'm glad things worked out for us."

If your partner is not respecting your feelings, it is time to get out of the relationship.

"Sara and I have been dating for two months," said Tom. "I love to be with her. She's funny and smart, and we have a lot of interests in common. But about two weeks ago she started asking me to sleep with her. I'm not ready to be sexually active. And now I don't know whether I want to stay with her.

"On the one hand, I really enjoy spending time with her. We have fun together, and she makes me happy. I feel good about myself when I'm with her—or at least I did until she started the sexual pressure.

"I do wish we could continue our relationship. But I'll stay with her only if she stops the pressure. I'm going to talk to her and see how she reacts."

If your partner is putting sexual pressure on you, you need to decide whether or not to stay in the relationship.

How do you feel about your partner? Do you think he or she will respect your feelings?

What are the benefits of staying in the relationship? Your partner has probably become a very special person in your life. The two of you may have the same hobbies or interests. You enjoy spending time together—going to the movies, taking a walk, or just talking.

What are the disadvantages of staying? Does your partner's sexual behavior make you very uncomfortable? Is the sexual pressure starting to take over the good parts of your relationship? How much anxiety do you feel when you are with your partner?

If your partner makes you too uncomfortable, it is probably time for you to get out. But you may decide you want to try to work things out. If so, you need to figure out how to negotiate.

Before you approach your partner, it is important to be clear about what you want. Think about your values and your limits. If your partner is putting sexual pressure on you, make sure you know what is making you uncomfortable. The more definite you are about what you want, the better able you will be to communicate effectively and negotiate with your partner.

Techniques for Saying No

You know your values and have established
your boundaries. You know what you need to
say to your partner—now how do you say it?

The best approach is to be straightforward and
direct. Setting your limits early will help you avoid
trouble later. Talk to your partner about why you
don't want to have sex. Explain how you feel. You
don't have to lie or make excuses. Telling the truth
is best. But even if you set your boundaries early,
you may still encounter sexual pressure later.

*"Ethan kept pressuring me to sleep with him," said
Tanya. "Finally I couldn't stand it anymore. I decided
that we had to sit down and talk or else I couldn't
continue the relationship.*

*"I told him that he was making me very uncomfort-
able. I don't want to have sex now, and I couldn't
really enjoy being with him anymore. The sexual pressure was making me too upset.*

*"I was surprised at his reaction. He told me he
wasn't ready for sex yet either, but he thought I would
think less of him if we didn't go all the way. Once we
had discussed it openly, our relationship was much
better. Neither one of us felt we were doing anything we
didn't want to do. And Ethan was actually relieved.
He knew he didn't have to put on an act or do anything that didn't feel right."*

Being honest and direct is the best approach when dealing with sexual pressure.

"I was nervous about saying no to Lisa," said Gabriel. "She kept pressuring me and pressuring me. Finally I talked to my brother. He told me I should just tell her I wasn't ready. If she couldn't handle that, it was time for us to go our separate ways.

"I finally got up the courage to tell her how I felt. She was really angry and wouldn't talk to me for a while. But after a few weeks she called me on the phone. She told me she had thought about what I said, and she respected me for my choice. She still wants to have sex, but she knows I don't. So for now we're not going to sleep together."

If you want to go more slowly than your partner, tell him or her your limits. You might say, "I really like kissing you and hugging you. But that's as far as I'm willing to go. Anything more makes me uncomfortable." You should go at your own pace.

"I really like spending time with Wayne," said Allison. "And I like kissing him or holding hands. But I'm not ready to go further than that. When he tried to get me to go to bed with him, I was completely honest.

"I said, 'Wayne, I don't want to get pregnant or get AIDS. And even if we use birth control, I'm just not ready to have sex yet. I want to wait until I get married.'

"I thought Wayne would dump me, but he was

really cool about it. I think he understood how I felt, and he told me he was glad I explained how I felt. He said a lot of girls aren't so honest. They just sort of play along and send all kinds of messages. Then he doesn't know how to react to them."

Here are some ways you might explain to your partner why you are saying no:

- "I'm worried about getting AIDS or other diseases."
- "I'm not ready to be a parent yet, and I don't want to take the risk of becoming one."
- "I really like you, but sex isn't a priority for me right now. I want to wait until I'm older."
- "I want to make absolutely sure I'm ready, and I'm still deciding."
- "According to my religious upbringing, sex before marriage is wrong. I hope you can respect my beliefs."
- "My parents are really strict, and they'd kill me if they found out."

Avoiding Sexual Pressure

You can try to avoid getting into situations where sexual pressure is likely to get out of control. Stay away from parties where there is heavy drinking or drug use. Using alcohol and other drugs can impair your judgment and you may do things you

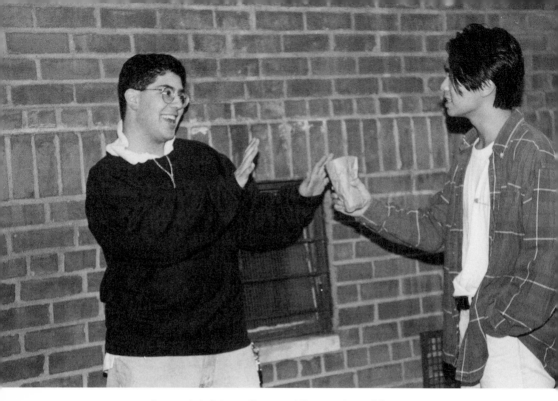
Drugs and alcohol can affect your ability to make good decisions.

wouldn't do if you were sober. This can lead to dangerous consequences.

- One study of teenagers with unintended pregnancies found that almost half had been drinking or using drugs before they engaged in the act of intercourse that led to the pregnancy.
- Another study found that sexually active teens who drink and/or use drugs used condoms 16 percent less often after drinking and 25 percent less often after using other drugs.
- A survey of college students found that 75 percent of the males and more than half of the females involved in date rape had been drinking or using other drugs before the attack.

If you are on a date with someone new, go to a place where there will be other people around, like a movie theater or a restaurant.

If you plan to attend a party where you don't know many of the guests, go with a friend so that the two of you can look out for each other.

Always let someone else know when you are going on a date, and make sure you have a way of getting home if you decide it's not working out. If you can't drive, call a relative, a friend, or a taxi. If you think you are in danger, contact the police right away.

Remember that you always have the right to say no to sexual pressure. Once you can do that, you will find that there are many advantages to being in control.

Staying in control will help you to feel strong and confident.

5 The Advantages of Being in Control

"CHARLIE AND I DECIDED VERY EARLY ON THAT we wouldn't have sex at all," said Liz. "Now we have a chance to enjoy each other without worrying about anything else.

"We go to the movies or take walks together— and basically just hang out. I really like to be with him. I feel good about our relationship since we decided right away how we would handle the sex issue. Now we can concentrate on enjoying our time together instead."

Liz and Charlie have both decided to stay in control in their relationship. And they are gaining many benefits. Each of them established clear boundaries at the beginning of their relationship. Now they can be sure that they are doing what they want to do. Neither partner feels pressured, and they have the opportunity to enjoy the non-sexual aspects of dating.

Stu asked Pam to go to the junior prom. Pam was really excited—and scared. She had always been shy, and she hadn't dated much before. Pam was afraid Stu might not think she was experienced or exciting enough. She thought she might like to kiss him. But what should she do if he asked her to do more?

Stu and Pam had a great time at the dance. After they left the prom, Stu took Pam for a drive. He stopped the car and started to kiss her. Then he asked her if he could unbutton her dress.

"I was really nervous," said Pam. "I didn't want to go further sexually, and I was afraid he would get angry or just leave me by the side of the road. But I decided that I had to do what I felt was right. I told him that he had to stop.

"And you know what? He respected what I said. He didn't try to go any further.

"I really felt good about myself. I stayed in control that night. And we've continued to date.

"I'm glad I was able to say no. I have more confidence in myself. I know I can do what feels right for me, no matter what kind of sexual pressure anyone might try to put on me."

When you are in a relationship, you share a part of yourself with another person. But you should also be able to maintain your own identity and know what is important to you. When you can say

You may prefer to be alone rather than be with someone who makes you feel pressured.

no to sexual pressure, you remain in control.

Being able to say no improves your confidence and makes you feel better about yourself. You can get more enjoyment out of your relationship since you won't be doing anything you're not ready for. You won't resent your boyfriend or girlfriend for making you do something you don't want to do. And you won't be upset with yourself for making a mistake you'll regret later.

Your self-esteem will be high because of your ability to trust yourself. If you have self-confidence about your sexual choices, you know that you can also make good decisions in other areas of your life.

"It seemed like every guy I went out with expected me to sleep with him," said Alicia. "One guy even had the nerve to say that it was okay if I didn't sleep with him, but he planned to tell his friends that we had done it because they would think it was weird if we hadn't! I said that was crazy. If he didn't feel like it would be cool to go out with me unless we were sleeping together, then he wasn't going to have the honor of going out with me at all. I'm going to wait until the guys my age are more mature. Right now, none of them seem to be able to handle dating without sex.

"Since I made my decision not to date right now, I've had a lot more time and energy for other things,

like my interest in student government. I'm also able to spend more time with friends—both male and female. They all helped me to organize a campaign for student body president. I won the election by a landslide! I'm so busy now with my new responsibilities that I can't imagine having time for a boyfriend. The weird thing is, I'm getting asked out more than ever! But being alone is really giving me the chance to figure out who I am. When the right guy comes along and I do decide to date again, I'll be able to bring a lot more to the relationship."

Learning to say no to sexual pressure is a big step toward becoming a responsible adult. You have shown that you can make wise choices about what you think is best for you.

Sexual pressure is one of the most difficult things teenagers deal with. It's hard to turn someone down, especially when it's someone you really like. You may be made to feel that you're being uptight or a prude. This is only because the person is feeling defensive and insecure about his or her own actions. People who put sexual pressure on others are usually feeling some sort of pressure themselves. Remind your partner that sexual involvement carries many risks, both emotional and physical.

Giving in to sexual pressure before you're ready

may not seem like a big deal now, but it can get a lot more complicated if you contract HIV, the virus that causes AIDS, or another sexually transmitted disease, or if you find yourself faced with an unintended pregnancy. Being sexually intimate with someone before you're ready can also hurt your relationship, leaving you both feeling guilty, uncertain, even angry.

If you can say no to sexual pressure, you have an important tool for protecting yourself.

Your decisions about your sexual behavior now and in the future will be good ones because they will reflect what you think is important. And you will develop good relationships because you will be able to relate well with others while staying in control of your body and your life.

Glossary

abstinence The act of refraining from having sexual intercourse.

AIDS (Acquired Immunodeficiency Syndrome) Deadly viral disease that may be spread by sexual contact, intravenous drug use, or the exchange of bodily fluids, including blood, semen, and vaginal secretions.

contraception Methods of birth control; ways of avoiding pregnancy, including condoms, birth control pills, diaphragms, and other methods.

date rape (acquaintance rape) Forcible sexual intercourse carried out by someone who knows the victim. The criminal may be a boyfriend/girlfriend, an acquaintance, or a friend of the victim.

gonorrhea A sexually transmitted disease that causes a swelling of the genital mucous membranes.

herpes A sexually transmitted disease with symptoms that include clusters of blisters on the mouth, skin, or genitals.

peer pressure Attempts by friends, classmates, or acquaintances to persuade a person to engage in certain behavior.

prude A person who is unusually modest.

rape The act of forcing someone to have sexual intercourse against his or her will. Rape is a crime of violence.

sexual pressure Verbal or physical attempts to persuade someone to engage in sexual activity.

sexually transmitted disease (STD) One of several disorders, such as syphilis, chlamydia, gonorrhea, herpes, and AIDS, that a person can catch from a sexual partner.

Help List

Advocates for Youth
1025 Vermont Avenue, NW, Suite 200
Washington, DC 20005
(202) 347-5700

KidSource Online Teen Pregnancy Prevention Site
Web site: http://www.kidsource.com/kidsource/content/
    news/teen_pregnancy.5.9.html

National AIDS Hot Line
(800) 342-2437

National Teen Pregnancy Clock
Web site: http://www.cfoc.org/clock.html

National Youth Crisis Hot Line
(800) 448-4663

Planned Parenthood Federation of America
810 Seventh Avenue
New York, NY 10019
(212) 541-7800
e-mail: communications@ppfa.org
Web site: http://www.ppfa.org/ppfa/

Sexuality Information and Education Council of the
    United States (SIECUS)
130 West 42nd Street
New York, NY 10036
(212) 879-1990

Teen Pregnancy Prevention and Intervention Program
Web site: http://goldmine.cde.ca.gov/www/lsp/
    teenhome.html

In Canada:

Planned Parenthood Federation of Canada
1 Nicholas Street, Suite 430
Ottawa, Ontario K1N 7B7
(613) 241-4474

For Further Reading

Bell, Ruth, et al. *Changing Bodies, Changing Lives: A Book for Teens on Sex and Relationships*. New York: Random House, 1987.

Benedict, Helen. *Safe, Strong, and Streetwise*. Boston: Little, Brown, 1987.

Beneke, Timothy. *Men on Rape: What They Have to Say About Sexual Violence*. New York: St. Martin's Press, 1982.

Berlfein, Judy. *Teen Pregnancy*. San Diego: Lucent Books, 1992.

Bode, Janet. *Kids Having Kids: People Talk About Teen Pregnancy*. New York: Franklin Watts, 1992.

Boston Women's Health Book Collective. *The New Our Bodies, Ourselves*. New York: Simon & Schuster, 1992.

Fenwick, Elizabeth, and Richard Walker. *How Sex Works*. New York: Dorling Kindersley Publishing, 1994.

Fiedler, Jean, and Hal Fiedler. *Be Smart About Sex*. Hillside, NJ: Enslow Publishers, 1990.

The Get Prepared Library of Violence Prevention for

Young Women. 8 vols. New York: Rosen Publishing Group, 1995.

Madaras, Lynda. *My Body, My Self.* New York: Newmarket Press, 1995.

Rozakis, Laurie. *Teen Pregnancy: Why Are Kids Having Babies?* New York: Twenty-First Century Books, 1993.

Zinner, Stephen. *How to Protect Yourself from STDs.* New York: Summit Books, 1986.

Index

About the Author
Anna Kreiner was born and raised in the Philadelphia area and received a master's degree in public health from the University of California at Los Angeles.

Photo Credits
Cover by Guillermina de Ferrari; pp. 27, 29 by Ira Fox; p. 42 by Yung-Hee Chia. All other photos by Guillermina de Ferrari.

Layout and Design
Erin McKenna